PHOTOSHOP AND WEB DESIGN BASICS FOR KIDS

TECHNOLOGY BOOK FOR KIDS

CHILDREN'S COMPUTER & TECHNOLOGY BOOKS

BABY PROFESSOR
EDUCATION KIDS

Speedy Publishing LLC
40 E. Main St. #1156
Newark, DE 19711
www.speedypublishing.com

Are you interested in learning how to create images for the web and how to create web designs? In this book, you will learn how to get started and what you will need.

Selection
Opacity :
100 %
BRANDI
STAR
Colour/49
FLAT COLOUR
INSPIRATION
Option
381.2455
88.462

Link
Play
Navigator   Rank Position   Void Ex
Over View
Side View
Bottom View
Top View
Perspective View
Grid View
Transparency View
X   76
Y   53
Z   51
Color   Tone   Symbols
43
68
47
71
Section Mark
42
83
34
Assign Point
38   2
69   54
21   41
40   81
cm
7 cm
1.05 cm
4.45 cm
17.07 cm
20 cm
75 cm
75°
155°
50.05 cm
TUP
SKETCH 1/17

For web designers, starting out young is very vital and advantageous. You get to learn without any prior knowledge or biases. We could easily compare teaching web design to a child to writing on a blank sheet of paper.

You can write without being distracted by previous doodles and scribbles. You can easily understand what you are writing because the paper is very clean; it has all the space in the world for your convenience.

Web designer working

Hence, like writing on a blank sheet of paper, teaching a kid to design websites could be a very satisfying experience. At one point, for our web designers out there, this is a perfect bonding opportunity with your son, daughter, younger brother or your toddler neighbor. You'll be able to hit two birds with one stone. You can work while teaching your kid a new cool hobby.

Web designer working

WEBPAGE
Effect
— Blur
— Speed
PLAY LIST !
② SELECT FILE.
DESKTOP
OPEN
* ① COVER
② WORDS
UPLOAD

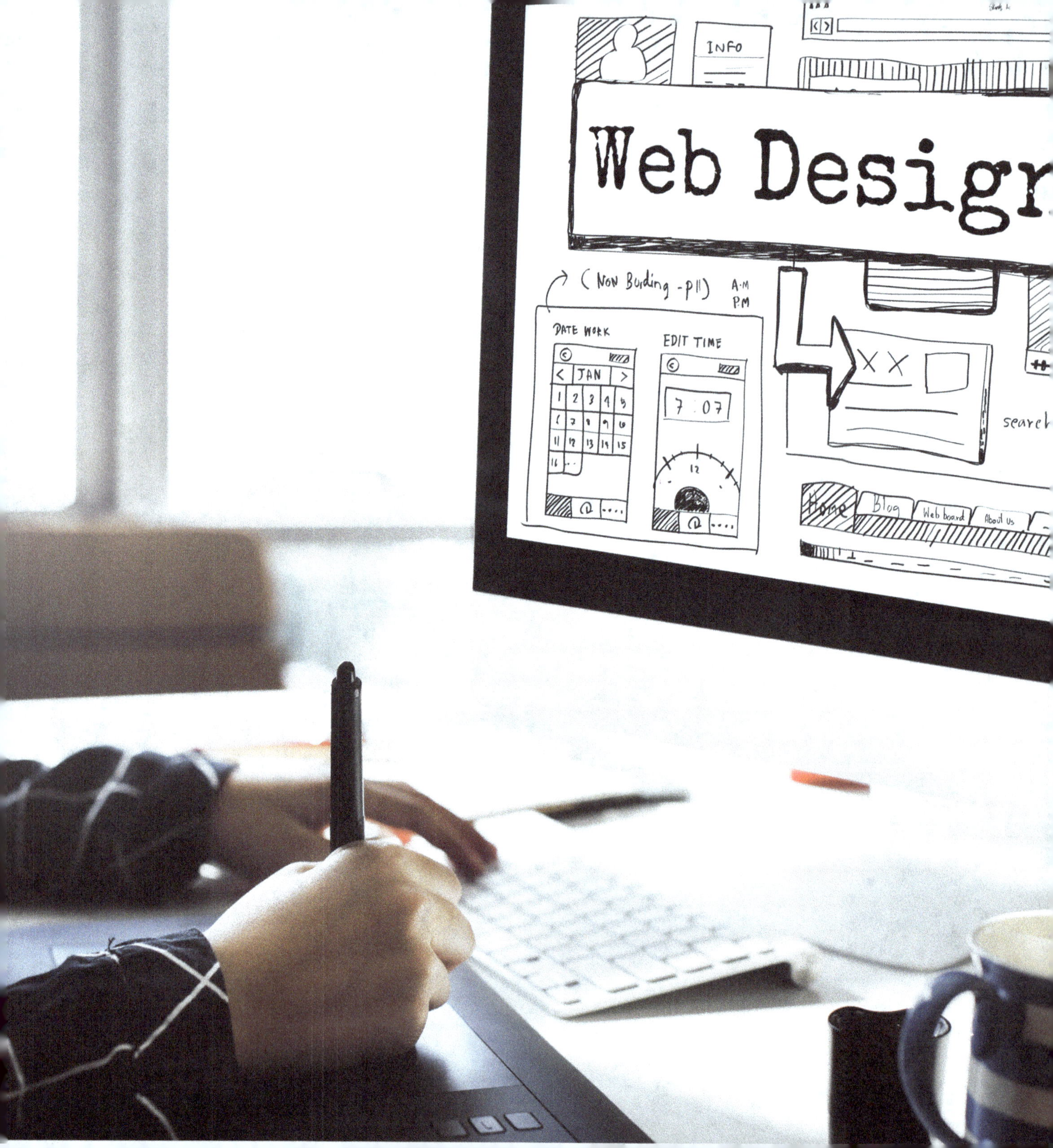

INFO
Web Design
(Non Binding - p.11)
A.M
P.M
DATE WORK
EDIT TIME
JAN
7 : 07
12
search
Home
Blog
Web board
About Us

The idea of kids designing and coding seems to perplex a lot of people. Some might be puzzled if they can really design and code fabulous websites with all the complicated tools and languages out there. Well, the thing is, this hobby will not go beyond the reach of a toddler's mind. It will just prepare them for the big thing. It's like teaching how to ride a bike using support wheels. Nevertheless, this is a good start.

Web Designer working on new web template

INFO
Web Des
(NON Burding -P II)
A·M
P·M
EDIT TIME

gn
search :
Keywords ...
About Us
Send

Like any other teaching endeavor, this activity will need necessary preparations. So, here they are:

CONDITION

The first thing you need to do in teaching your kid how to design webpages is to condition their minds to the work. Expose them to computers, web pages, and the workplace. You need to make them aware where they are and what is supposed to be done whenever they are at that place.

Try to show some graphic designs that you created yourself. Let the child ask about anything, no matter how complicated it may seem. Remember, exposure leads to experience and experience leads to excellence. Just let them be there, and observe. Children are naturally curious, and soon enough, they'll find answers. Next thing you'll know, your child will immerse himself/herself in the work.

Web layout sketch

You could start conditioning their minds by letting them design what they want. Say, they are very interested in robots, then start by creating a robot related mock-up. Tell the child about how every element of the design looks and functions like a part of a robot.

Take them to the workplace. I'm sure when they frequently visit the place, they will soon become curious about what you do. Eventually, you will see them peeking at your monitor and then sitting beside your lap and starting asking questions.

Web Designer working

You could also talk to them about web design a lot. Talking breeds admiration and soon breeds inspiration. If they could see that you are having fun with the job, they will give it a try.

Creative Briefing
Research
Sketch & Design
Presentation
Feedback
CREATIVE PROCESS
Corrections to
Selected Concepts
Final Presentation
Files Delivery
Launch!

WEBSIT
CONVERT FILE
+
8
② SELECT FILE.
DESKTOP
OPEN
* ① COVER
② WORDS
10
20
30
50
RESEARE

LAYOUT

TAKE IT SLOW

Taking it slow does not only apply to romantic relationships. It also is accepted in teaching kids. As a web design teacher, I am sure you will be pretty much hasty to see your student perform web miracles. But that's not going to happen. Learning is a process. Start with the basics. Teach them the elements of web design, then the tools, then codes and so on. Just let them digest everything. Remember, you're talking with a toddler, not a programming god.

Website designer working with digital tablet and computer laptop

WEB DESIGN
Effect
- Blur
- Speed
SELECT FILE
PLAY LIST !
PLAY LIST
UPLOAD
30%
CONVERT FILE
COVER
WORDS
TYPE I
TYPE

People who have messed with this stage suffered grave setbacks. They rushed into teaching advanced stuff to kids, and the kids ended up disinterested. Remember that the attention span of a child is very narrow, so might as well sustain it slowly than go fast and crash.

Web designer at work

HTML5
Layout
resposive WEB
text design
fonts usability
prototype CSS3
perfect
UI px website
em
icons pages
content
images UX

Remember the basics of web design. Wireframing, designing the layout, coding the HTML, CSS, PHP and Java scripts, and then content creation.

For more info, you could visit:

- How to Build a Blog – Ultimate Guide for Beginners

- Beginner's Guide to Wireframes and Tools to Create Them

- Working with Types: Typography Design Tutorial for Beginners

- Basic Web Design Video Course – Wireframing, Photoshop Tools & Panels, and Designing [Part 1]

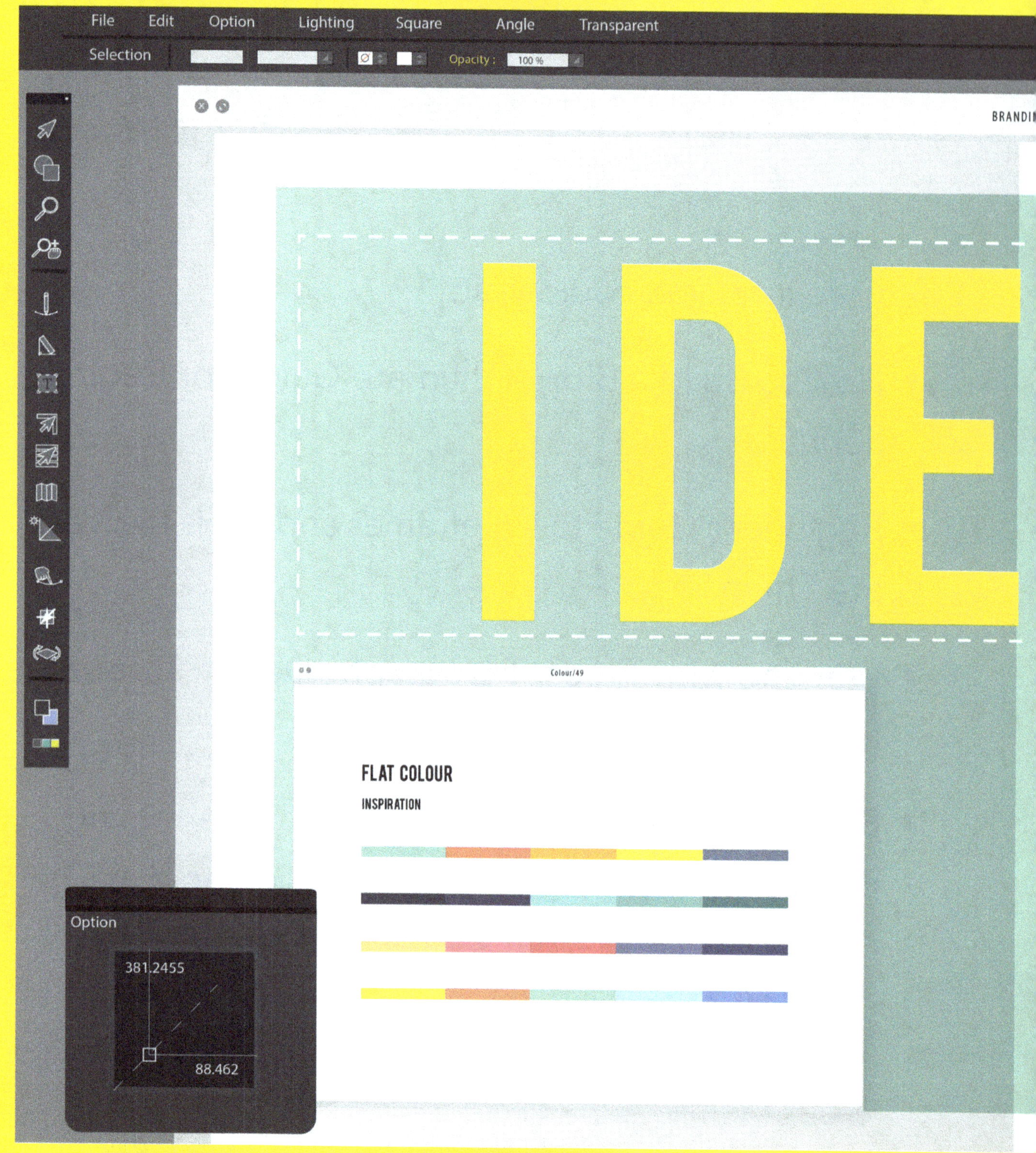
File
Edit
Option
Lighting
Square
Angle
Transparent
Selection
Opacity :
100 %
BRANDI
IDE
Colour/49
FLAT COLOUR
INSPIRATION
Option
381.2455
88.462

Link
Play
Navigator   Rank Position   Void Ex
Over View
Side View
Bottom View
Top View
Perspective View
Grid View
Transparency View
X   76
Y   53
Z   51
Color   Tone   Symbols
43
68
47
71
Section Mark
42
83
34
Assign Point
38   2
69   54
21   41
7 cm
15.05 cm
4.45 cm
17.07 cm
75 cm
20 cm
50.05 cm
SKETCH 1/17

STOOP DOWN

Let's admit it, HTML, CSS and other programming languages could be crazy at first glance. In fact, it may just look like a bunch of letters and characters all thrown together when you look at it. And that's what you need to consider when teaching a kid to design websites. You need to make things simple for him.

Stoop down to his level and make him understand. You need not to sound smart with them, you just need to sound believable. Remember, what kids do not understand, they won't do.

B DESIGN
CH #2
LOGO
catego
x5
COMPANY
5000 px
ABOUT US
contact info
corporate graphic
responsive design
for mobile

Use simple words. Try to analogize the terms into something that they will find interest in. Example, you may analogize an .img .src tag to an aim targeted by a bowman. Relate to their likes, interests; movies watched, TV shows and a lot more. Remember, sounding smart to a kid is still sounding dumb to them. Be at their playful curious and mischievous age.

> Develop

```
// persisted properties

<html> <p style="font-weight:bold;">HTML font code is done using CSS.</p>
<html> <body style="background-color:yellowgreen;color:white;">
<html> <.todolistid = data.todoidb;


// Non - persisted properties
  <html> <errorMessage = ko , observable() ;


<p style="color:orange;">HTML font code is done using CSS.</p>

  function  todoitem(data) { ;
    var  self = this ;
    data = dta  ll { } ;

<p>You can make <span style="font-style:italic">some</span> the HTML 'span' tag.
<p>You can bold <span style="">parts</span> of your text using the HTML tag.</p>


<html> <p style="font-weight:bold;"
>HTML font code is done using CSS.</p>
<html> <body style="background-
color:yellowgreen;
color:white;">
<html> <.todolistid = data.todoidb;
```

Graphic/Web Designer workstation

IDEAS
AT
9
A

TOOLS

It seems implausible that someone will learn web design if he doesn't have any computer. In fact, that would be next to impossible for a web designer to learn more from books than from sitting in front of the computer for hours.

Photoshop icon on laptop screen

Like any other hobby, web designing requires tools. Your children will need the same. As starting web designers, you have to equip them with the necessary gadgets or platforms where they can start learning.

Creative Cloud app icon

Photos
Creative Cloud

Close-up of working place of designer

Buy a computer. Install some basic programming games. Make it fun so that when the time comes for the kid to roll, the job will be more fun.

Here are some tools and games you could use:

- Scratch

- Stencyl

Selection
Opacity : 100 %
Colour/49
DES
FLAT COLOUR
INSPIRATION
Option
381.2455
88.462

Link
Play
Navigator   Rank Position   Void Ex
Over Vie
Side Vie
Bottom
Top Vie
Perspe
Grid Vie
Transpa
X
Y
Z
Color   Tone   Symbols
Section Mark
42
83
34
Assign Point
38   2
69   54
21   41
GN
28 cm
7.05 cm
7 cm
4.45 cm
17.07 cm
.75 cm
20 cm
50.05 cm
SKETCH 1/17

Here are some tips:

- Show them the basic elements of a browser and which browsers is recommended.

- Explain what links, texts, images and other elements are. Be sure to differentiate each to them.

- Explain what HTML and CSS do.

- Orient them with the basic language of the two platforms (HTML and CSS).

- Orient them with various editors like GIMP, Paint, Photoshop (this is very advanced) and others. Let them use their thinking caps young!

Online Learning Center E-learning Library Concept

Hen
THE CHICKEN
LIFE CYCLE
Adult chicken
Eggs
Chick
Hatching
THE CHICKEN
LIFE CYCLE
Hen
Adult chicken
Eggs
Chick
Hatching

CONCLUSION

Web designing is a pretty cool hobby. In fact, it's a hobby where you could earn some money. Now with you teaching your kid on how to design websites, you are thereby exposing them to the kind of work they might want to do someday. It gives them the edge above others since he is very familiar with the profession.

Thus, you are not only securing a job as a designer, but you are also establishing the bond with your child and preparing him for a possible career. And besides, you've got nothing to lose with your kids. Everything is a gain.

Visit
BABY PROFESSOR
EDUCATION KIDS
www.BabyProfessorBooks.com
to download Free Baby Professor eBooks
and view our catalog of new and exciting
Children's Books